05

D1344853

hen

butterflies

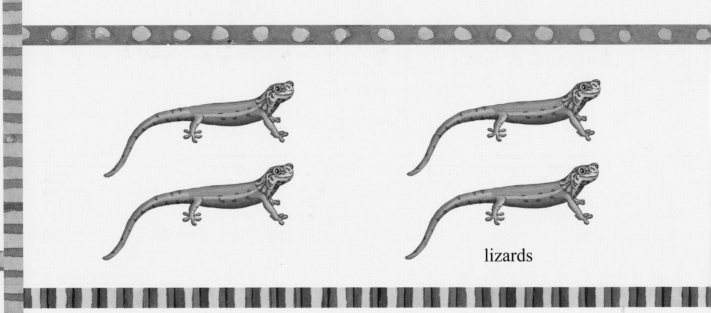

mice

lizards

sunbirds

crickets

baby bullfrogs

spoonbills

starlings

For John and Milo

The children featured in this book are from the Luo tribe of south-west Kenya.

The wild creatures are the Citrus Swallowtail (butterfly), Striped Grass Mouse,
Yellow-headed Dwarf Gecko, Beautiful Sunbird, Armoured Ground Cricket,
(young) African Bullfrog, African Spoonbill and Superb Starling.

The author would like to thank everyone who helped her research this book,
in particular Joseph Ngetich from the Agricultural Office of the Kenya High Commission.

Text and illustrations copyright © 2002 Eileen Browne
Dual Language copyright © 2003 Mantra Lingua
This edition published 2003
Published by arrangement with Walker Books Limited
London SE11 5HJ

British Library Cataloguing in Publication Data:
a catalogue record for this book is available from the British Library.

Published by
Mantra Lingua
5 Alexandra Grove, London N12 8NU
www.mantralingua.com

دجاجة هاندا

Handa's Hen

Eileen Browne

Arabic translation by Dr Sajida Fawzi

mantra

كان لجدة هاندا دجاجة واحدة سوداء اسمها موندي
وكانت موندي تطعمها وجبة الفطور صباح كل يوم.

Handa's grandma had one black hen.
Her name was Mondi - and every morning
Handa gave Mondi her breakfast.

وفي احد الأيام لم تكن موندي موجودة في موعد فطورها.

نادت هاندا قائلة "جدتي! هل ترين موندي حولك؟"

"لا، ولكني آرى صديقتك." اجابت جدتها.

"اكِيو! ساعديني في ايجاد موندي." قالت هاندا.

One day, Mondi didn't come for her food. "Grandma!" called Handa. "Can you see Mondi?"

"No," said Grandma. "But I can see your friend."

"Akeyo!" said Handa. "Help me find Mondi."

وفتشت هاندا واكِيو في بيت الدجاج .
"أنظري ! فراشتان مرفرفتان" قالت اكِيو .
"ولكن أين موندي؟" قالت هاندا .

Handa and Akeyo hunted round the hen house.
"Look! Two fluttery butterflies," said Akeyo.
"But where's Mondi?" said Handa.

ونظرتا تحت مخزن الحبوب.
"هشششش! ثلاثة فئران مُقلّمة اللون "قالت اكِيو.
"ولكن أين موندي؟" قالت هاندا.

They peered under a grain store.
"Shh! Three stripy mice," said Akeyo.
"But where's Mondi?" said Handa.

واختلستا النظر خلف الجرار.
"أرى اربع سحالي" قالت أَكِيو.
"ولكن أين موندي؟" قالت هوندا.

They peeped behind some clay pots.
"I can see four little lizards," said Akeyo.
"But where's Mondi?" said Handa.

وفتشتا حول بعض الأشجار المزهرة.
"هناك خمسة من طيور التُمَيْر الجميلة" قالت أكِيو.
"ولكن أين موندي؟" قالت هاندا.

They searched round some flowering trees.
"Five beautiful sunbirds," said Akeyo.
"But where's Mondi?" said Handa.

وفتِشتا بين اِلحشيش المتمايِل.
"هناك ستة من صراصير الليل! لنصطادهم" قالت أكِيو.
"اريد أن أجدَ موندي" قالت هاندا.

They looked in the long, waving grass.
"Six jumpy crickets!" said Akeyo. "Let's catch them."
"I want to find Mondi," said Handa.

وذهبتا بعيداً الى منبع الماء.

"هناك سبعة من صغار الضفادع!" قالت أكِيو.

They went all the way down to the water hole.
"Baby bullfrogs," said Akeyo. "There are seven!"

"ولكن أين...آه أنظري! بصمات قدم!" قالت هوندا.
وتعقّبوا الأثر ووجدوا...

"But where's … oh look! Footprints!" said Handa.
They followed the footprints and found …

"لَقالق ملعقية المنقار لا غير، سبعة منها...لا ثمانية، قالت هاندا."

"ولكن أين، اووه أين موندي؟"

"Only spoonbills," said Handa. "Seven … no, eight.
But where, oh where is Mondi?"

" ارجو الّا يكون قد ابتلعها اللقلق الملعقي
المنقار أو قد أكلها أسد " قالت أكِيو .

"I hope she hasn't been swallowed by a spoonbill -
or eaten by a lion," said Akeyo.

واتّجهتا حزينتين في طريقهما الى الجدّة.
"هناك تسعة زرازير برّاقة اللون" قالت أَكِيو.

Feeling sad, they went back towards Grandma's.
"Nine shiny starlings - over there!" said Akeyo.

"اسمعي،" جيب جيب "ما هذا الصوت؟" قالت هاندا.

جيب جيب جيب جيب جيب جيب جيب

"إنه قادم من تحت تلك الشجرة الصغيرة. دعينا نختلس النظر تحتها؟"

"Listen," said Handa. cheep cheep "What's that?"

cheep cheep cheep cheep cheep cheep cheep cheep

"It's coming from under that bush. Shall we peep?"

هاندا، أَكِيو، موندي وعشرة كتاكِيت.

Handa, Akeyo, Mondi and ten chicks

اتّجهوا جميعاً عائدين الى الجدّة تارةً يُسرعون وتارةً يقفزون...

hurried and scurried and skipped back to Grandma's ...

وأكلوا جميعاً وجبة الفطور في وقت متأخر جداً.

where they all had a very late breakfast.

hen

mice

lizards

butterflies

sunbirds

crickets

baby bullfrogs

spoonbills

starlings

chicks

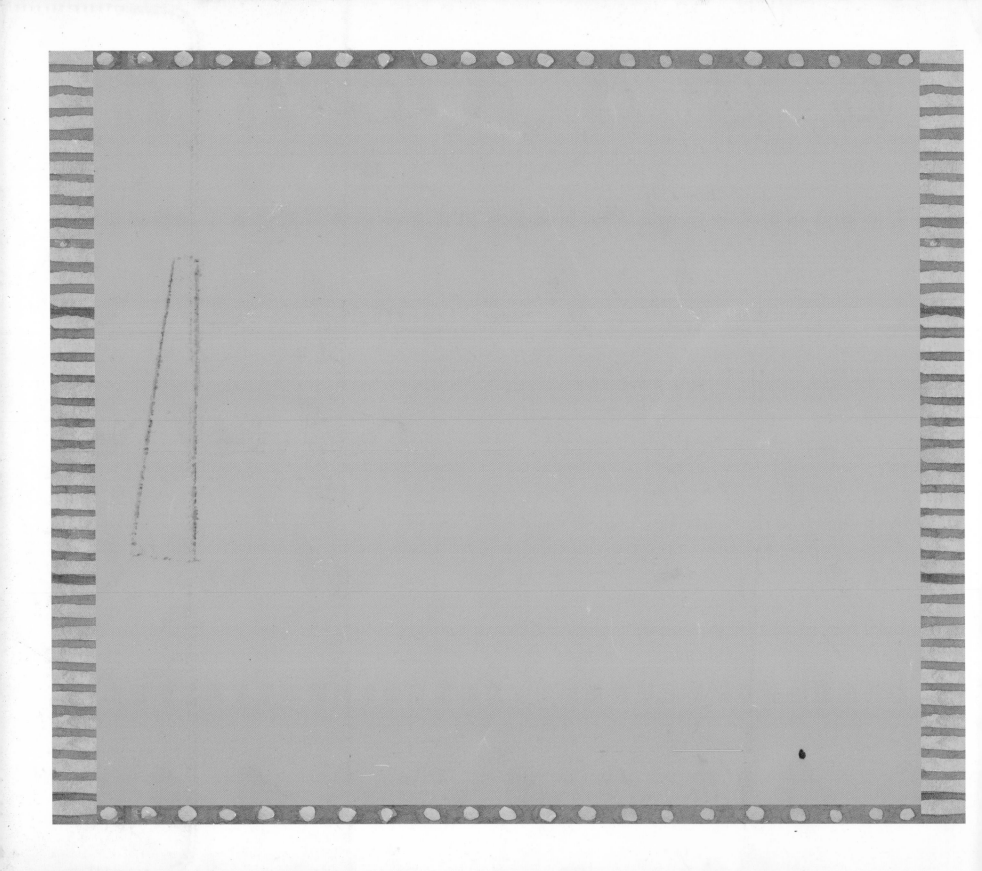